# CONTENTS

# MEET THE IDIOTS!

As the world's worst life coach, people never ask me to recommend anything. But if they did, this book would be top of my list.

Other illustrated books may offer wholesome platitudes from talking horses and weird moles, but this one is an entirely different beast.

World history has been changed by many famous quartets, like The Beatles, The Rolling Stones and The Three Musketeers; and the unlikely characters at the heart of this story are equally memorable.

*The Boomer is a miserable old git.*

The smug, world-weary Boomer, with his paid-off mortgage, triple-locked pension, and contempt for all  that is woke is a perfect foil to the self-righteous, virtue-signalling Snowflake, with principles so unshakeable you could practically stub your toe on them.

*The Snowflake is permanently offended.*

But these two human culture warriors are set off wonderfully by the violent, impulsive Baboon, absolutely brimming with animal vitality.

*The Baboon is a hairy great menace.*

And the wistful, painfully optimistic Stuffed Dodo, which clearly isn't.

*The Stuffed Dodo doesn't have a lot going for it.*

Like an angry, incoherent drunk, barely keeping his balance after twelve pints too many, the author skilfully weaves a confusing narrative into a ludicrous ramble, and the accompanying illustrations are so rough and ready, they make South Park look like an animated version of The Sistene Chapel.

Every prison libarary should have a copy!

Cuthbert Huntsman, Broadmoor, 2025.
www.cuthberthuntsman.com

# THE BIN FIRE

"Let's start a bin fire!" exclaimed The Baboon as it swung off a bus stop.

The Snowflake shook her head. "What about health and safety?"

"It might liven things up a bit." The Boomer handed The Baboon a box of matches.

The Stuffed Dodo didn't like flames; it was full of straw, after all. So it said, "Let me tell you a secret instead."

"Not again!" The Boomer groaned.

But there was no stopping The Stuffed Dodo. "I can fly." It smiled knowingly.

The Baboon, The Boomer and The Snowflake all looked at The Stuffed Dodo as it tensed up, closed its eyes and imagined its wings opening up as it launched into the sky.

In its head, The Stuffed Dodo swooped majestically over the Atlantic Ocean, looking down at the glistening ships, colourful yachts and cavorting whales far below.

But outside its head, nothing happened.

The Boomer looked at his watch. The Baboon yawned. The Snowflake empathised, but didn't do anything.

The Stuffed Dodo closed its eyes once again, let go of all of its fears, put its failures firmly in the past and imagined it was very brave indeed.

The Stuffed Dodo pictured itself sprinting along the ground, flapping its tiny, useless wings and zooming up, up, up above the clouds. It soared above aeroplanes and satellites, and eventually went into orbit. The Stuffed Dodo was in space!

Except it wasn't. The Stuffed Dodo was still planted to the ground, exactly where it had been.

"You can't fly, can you?" observed The Boomer.

"Don't be unkind!" The Snowflake hugged The Stuffed Dodo, who would have cried if its tear ducts hadn't been torn out by a taxidermist.

"Why not get real?" suggested The Boomer. "You are not just stuffed, you're extinct."

"But what about my mental health?" The Stuffed Dodo sniffed.

No one knew what to say, so The Baboon struck a match and set fire to the nearest bin.

# TRIGGERED

"Oi! You!" said The Baboon.

The Snowflake, The Boomer and The Stuffed Dodo all looked at each other, wondering if he meant them.

"You with the blue hair, vegan tattoos, pronoun pins, slogan t-shirt, and gender-neutral cargo pants!" continued The Baboon.

Everyone knew he meant The Snowflake.

But The Snowflake didn't mind. She thought it was important to debate people whose ideas were wrong. That way, they would soon come to realise that she was correct about everything and the world would be just right.

The Snowflake strode up to The Baboon and said, "I suppose you mean me."

"Who else, virtue-vampire?"

This was quite a big insult for a primate, but The Snowflake didn't feel like telling The Baboon this. Instead, The Snowflake simply said, "I find that really triggering."

"Triggering!" The Boomer echoed in a silly voice.

The Snowflake had not expected The Boomer to get involved, but he sometimes took exception to things.

The Snowlflake was about to give The Boomer a piece of her mind, when he reached into his pocket, pulled out a water pistol and squirted The Snowflake on the nose.

"How's *that* for triggering?" laughed The Boomer.

The Baboon scrunched up its face in a toothy grin, bobbed its head, thumped the ground and shook its big red butt in glee.

The Stuffed Dodo would have done the same, but it couldn't move.

"I thought this was a safe space!" The Snowflake squealed as she pointed repeatedly at The Boomer. She was very angry indeed, but her finger jabs just made it look like she was rubbish at invisible darts.

The Boomer squirted The Snowflake in the face once again, partly to prove that it was not a safe space and partly for the bants.

The Snowflake shrieked and stamped her feet. "You're so mean, and cruel and ..." She hesitated for a moment while her brain grasped for the worst word it could find. The word turned out to be "old!".

The Boomer burst into tears.

It convinced The Stuffed Dodo. The Snowflake wasn't sure, even though she liked to tell everyone she was an "empath". The Baboon, however, could tell that The Boomer was just having a laugh.

When The Boomer stopped pretending to cry, he turned to The Snowflake and said, "Surely calling someone old is mean and cruel?"

"It doesn't count," said The Snowflake. "You were punching down. I was punching up."

The Stuffed Dodo didn't think punching in any direction was a good idea, maybe because it didn't have any arms.

The Baboon had long, hairy arms and one of its favourite hobbies was punching. It hit the bus stop repeatedly, screeching and shouting, "Woo-ah! Ah!" again and again.

The Stuffed Dodo was not sure what "Woo-ah! Ah!" actually meant, but it didn't seem safe to ask.

The Snowflake had never punched anyone. She thought words could be much more hard-hitting, particularly if they were her own. So she said, "You are an old, privileged boomer from the nineteen hundreds. The twentieth century was toxic, and your attitudes are outdated. Everyone is equal now and everything is inclusive. Life is about caring, sensitivity and being right."

"Got any more platitudes?" asked The Boomer.

"More than an eagle's eye can see," said The Snowflake, irritatingly.

"Well, bleeding well keep them to yourself." The Boomer squirted a third jet of water into The Snowflake's face, and shuffled off to the betting shop.

# SHROOMS

One day, The Baboon, The Boomer, The Snowflake and The Stuffed Dodo went for a walk in the forest.

The Stuffed Dodo's legs were about as much use as a pair of chocolate teapots, so The Baboon had to carry it.

When they reached a clearing, The Baboon was starting to grow weary, so it dropped The Stuffed Dodo onto a cluster of mushrooms.

"You're a fat bastard!" said The Baboon, as it waved a long hairy arm at The Stuffed Dodo's straw belly.

"Don't body-shame the poor thing!" protested The Snowflake.

"It's a stuffed dodo," observed The Boomer.

The Stuffed Dodo knew it was a stuffed dodo, so it wasn't all that bothered. Besides, the mushrooms were quite comfortable.

The Snowflake was still indignant. She had to call someone out and make this what she liked to call a "teachable moment". The Baboon wasn't a great listener, so The Snowflake decided to lay into The Boomer. "What about all that cake you eat?"

"Cake!" The Boomer turned gammon-red. "What on Earth is wrong with cake?

"It's full of sugar and lard and carbs and it's destroying the planet," said The Snowflake.

The Stuffed Dodo couldn't work out how cake was destroying the planet, but it knew not to argue with The Snowflake. It didn't want to get cancelled.

"How about mushrooms?" The Baboon began chucking handfulls of the wild mushrooms at the other three, shouting "Woo-ah! Ah!"

The mushrooms didn't hurt, but they were extremely tasty, thought The Stuffed Dodo. Soon, it had scooped up six or seven of them into its beak.

The Boomer picked a spotty mushroom off his jacket and examined it closely. "I suppose it might be poisonous, but I'm absolutely famished." He gave it a nibble.

The Snowflake thought that The Boomer had already had what boomers like to call a "good innings", so if he did die of mushroom poisoning she would not have to pretend to be all that sad. But she was quite young, and had not had a "good innings", so she decided not to eat any mushrooms.

The Baboon didn't tend to think too much about things, so it gobbled handfulls of the wild fungi willy nilly.

It was not long before The Snowflake noticed that everyone else had gone cross-eyed. Had they all lost their minds?

Not entirely. Thanks to the mushrooms, their minds had simply taken them elsewhere.

The Baboon was swinging through a space jungle, where the trees were made of cake. It was delicious, but the Battenberg branches were too weak to support its weight and it kept falling off.

Luckily, the jungle floor was made of jelly, so it bounced back up to the trees. The Baboon wished all forests were like this.

The Boomer was on an all-inclusive cruise across the high seas. The ocean liner had a skull-and-crossbones flag and all the staff were pirates.

The passengers were in constant conversation with each other, but all anyone ever said was "Shiver me timbers."

The Stuffed Dodo was at a swingers' disco. Everyone seemed to like each other very much, and people kept offering him car keys.

The Stuffed Dodo found this all a bit odd, as it didn't drive.

The Snowflake was feeling left out, so she nibbled the corner of the smallest mushroom she could see. Nothing seemed to happen for several seconds, then the world changed. She was on a massive protest march in Trafalgar Square and everyone was carrying placards reading, "Equality.".

The police all wore paisley kilts and tartan tank tops and started chanting her name: "Snowflake! Snowflake! Snowflake!"

Before she knew it, the crowd had swept her off her feet and carried her to the base of Nelson's Column. The four bronze lions all gave her welcoming roars, sprouted wings and flew her to the top of the column.

At the top, Admiral Nelson opened his single remaining arm and hugged her to his chest. She looked down at the crowd a hundred and fifty feet below, and started giving one of the best speeches in the history of the world.

The Snowflake did not have a megaphone, but it didn't matter - the crowd could hear every word. "I am your new leader!" The Snowflake said. "And you are my subjects. I am in charge of everything that you do, and you are all completely equal."

The crowd applauded so hard, she fell off Nelson's Column and plunged down to Trafalgar Square.

But instead of dying in a cataclysmic splat, she found herself back in the clearing with The Baboon, The Boomer and The Stuffed Dodo.

Everyone's eyes had uncrossed, but they all looked rather discombobulated.

"That was emotional," said The Stuffed Dodo.

"Certainly blew away a few of the old cobwebs," said The Boomer.

"Let's take some more!" said The Baboon.

The Snowflake didn't want to. She had seen her future.

As The Baboon, The Boomer and The Stuffed Dodo walked back through the forest, they had no idea that The Snowflake was planning world domination.

# UNTRUE CRIME

It was a dank Saturday morning, so The Baboon, The Boomer, The Snowflake, and The Stuffed Dodo decided to visit the shops.

The town centre was busy and they attracted quite a few funny looks. Perhaps people were not used to seeing primates, pensioners, social justice warriors, and extinct, flightless birds looking for bargains.

All of a sudden, The Baboon stopped in the middle of the pavement, turned to the others, and said, "Let's start a podcast!"

"Let's not," said The Boomer.

"I'd love to be famous," said The Stuffed Dodo.

"You could go on *Strictly*," said The Boomer.

"Really?" The Stuffed Dodo's eyes blazed with excitement.

"No," said The Boomer. "You can't move, let alone dance."

"That's cruel," said The Snowflake. "What a mean thing to say!"

"Do you opinions matter to you?" asked The Boomer.

"Yes," replied The Snowflake indignantly.

"Well, I'm glad they matter to someone," said The Boomer.

"We could do a podcast about football!" said The Baboon.

"Or film criticism," said The Snowflake.

"Or celebrities," said The Stuffed Dodo.

"Or my bollocks," said The Boomer.

"Don't be crude," said The Snowflake.

"How about true crime?" suggested The Stuffed Dodo.

This gave The Baboon an idea.

"We could commit a crime!" said The Baboon. "Then we'd know it's definitely true!"

"I'm not sure that's a good idea," said The Snowflake.

But it was too late. The Baboon had already broken into a jewellery store and trousered all the Rolexes.

Alarms screamed, passers by looked ready to turn vigilante, and sirens blared in the surrounding streets.

The Baboon, The Boomer and The Snowflake ran off as quickly as they could.

The Snowflake legged it down a back street.

The Boomer sloped off down an alleyway.

The Baboon punched a traffic warden and ran across a car park.

But The Stuffed Dodo could not move. All it could do was wait
on the pavement, as police vans screeched to a halt, and heavily armed

officers forced it to the ground, before handcuffing its pitifully small wings.

Life could be tricky when you are extinct, mused The Stuffed Dodo as it was taken down the station.

# SPARRING

The Baboon, The Boomer, The Snowflake and The Stuffed Dodo had gone on a spa day. It was in a dodgy Hertfordshire hotel frequented by travelling businessmen and ladies of a professional disposition, but The Stuffed Dodo had made the booking without checking the reviews.

As our foursome exfoliated in the frankly unhygienic treatment room, The Stuffed Dodo decided to break the resentful silence by asking the others, "What do you want from life?"

"Fast cars, fast women and fast food," replied The Boomer.

"You can't say that!" said The Snowflake.

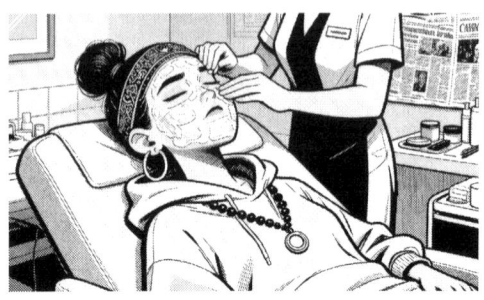

"I just did," said The Boomer.

"I want bananas, pies and fist fights," said The Baboon.

"But do they really make you happy?" asked The Stuffed Dodo.

"Fighting does," said The Baboon.

"Okay," said The Boomer. "Let's have a fight!".

"I'm a pacifist," said The Snowflake.

"I'm not all that quick on my feet," said The Stuffed Dodo.

"Fine," said The Boomer. "Looks like it's just us, hairy boy."

The Baboon and The Boomer got up from their exfoliation beds and let their towels drop.

Luckily, The Boomer was wearing swimming trunks, even though they were what people often called "budgie smugglers".

The Snowflake and The Stuffed Dodo watched as The Baboon thumped the floor.

The Boomer calmly got dressed, and tried to remember some of the dodgy moves he had learned in the Freemasons.

The Baboon stode towards The Boomer, beating its chest and shouting ""Woo-ah! Ah!". It had five times The Boomer's muscle strength and double his animal survival instinct, but The Boomer had a black belt in office politics.

"Look!" shouted The Boomer as he pointed at The Snowflake.

The Baboon turned, but The Snowflake was just lying there, exfoliating.

By the time The Baboon realised it had been tricked, The Boomer had kicked its hairy legs away from under it and left it lying upside down in a foot spa.

The Boomer laughed at the recumbent Baboon, and thought how lucky he had been to have joined a masonic lodge.

# DODO DREAMS

For reasons no one quite understood, The Baboon, The Boomer, The Snowflake and The Stuffed Dodo all lived in the dormitory wing of a tree house in the darkest depths of Epping Forest.

One night, as they lay in their beds struggling to get to sleep, The Stuffed Dodo asked, "What do you dream about?"

"A good night's sleep," replied The Boomer grumpily.

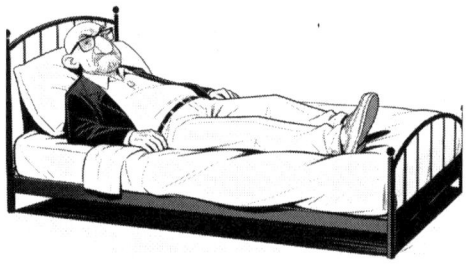

"World peace," said The Snowflake rather aggressively.

"Bananas," said The Baboon.

"I dream about Scotland," said The Stuffed Dodo. "I've always wanted to migrate to the Highlands."

"The Scottish Highlands are full of midges," said The Snowflake.

"And Scots," said The Boomer.

"Trees too," said The Baboon. "But no bananas,"

"It doesn't matter," said The Stuffed Dodo. "Just imagine flying over the glens! The castles! The lochs!"

"Watch out for monsters!" advised The Snowflake.

The Stuffed Dodo pictured Nessie, the mythical plesiosaur with its long neck, flippers, and snag-toothed smile, and decided that they would probably get on famously.

"How are you going to get there?" asked The Boomer.

It was a good point. Being stuffed had its limitations, particularly in the mobility department. "It's just a dream," said The Stuffed Dodo, but its mind took flight.

It pictured an entire flock of stuffed dodos soaring across the glorious Scottish skies, with the rugged landscape laid out below.

There were the Lowlands, with their multi-hued heathers. There were the Cairngorm mountains, with the indomitable Ben Nevis, and there was a grouse moor, with its tweedy shooters, blasting merrily at the sky.

One by one, the stuffed dodos fell from the heavens, to be collected by hungry but ultimately disappointed gamekeepers.

This wasn't a dream at all, it was a nightmare! The Stuffed Dodo shrieked through its beak and crash-landed in Loch Ness, where it was brutalised and swallowed whole by Nessie.

The Stuffed Dodo opened its eyes, looked at its friends in the tree house, and said, "Might give Scotland a miss this year."

# INFLUENCERS

"**I** want to be an influencer," said The Stuffed Dodo.

"You're too old," said The Snowflake.

"Exactly how old are you?" asked The Boomer.

The Stuffed Dodo had a long think. One day, it had been prancing around Mauritius without a care in the world. Then a bunch of sailors had turned up, chased it and filled its insides with straw.

The date had stuck in its mind: 14 February 1662. Valentine's Day! It would have been about thirteen.

After The Stuffed Dodo had told them this, The Baboon tried doing the sums, but it was too stupid to figure out the answer.

The Snowflake got her phone out, and put the numbers into an app.

But the Boomer beat her to it. "Three-hundred-and-seventy-six, give or take." He had been taught mental arithmetic at school and this made him very proud, even though it was largely useless in the 2020s.

"Is three-hundred-and-seventy-six really too old to be an influencer?" asked The Stuffed Dodo.

"Yes," said The Snowflake. "You need to be a digital native like me." This made The Stuffed Dodo feel sad.

The Snowflake noticed this and tried to make it feel better. "Maybe you could do a faceless YouTube channel."

"Or beakless," said The Boomer.

"I could post about bananas," said The Baboon.

"Branded banana content?" The Snowflake was intrigued. "That could work."

"Bollocks," said The Boomer. "Who brands bananas? Stupid yellow things that dangle all day."

"You could post about misery," said The Snowflake.

She hadn't meant to be encouraging, but The Boomer took it that way and went off on one, "Good thinking! Perhaps I could tell people what the world's really like. Instead of all these supermodels boasting about their posh lunches and luxury holidays, I could tell it like it is – back pain, knee replacement surgery, and disappointment."

"Who'd click on that?" asked The Snowflake.

This made The Boomer quite cross. "What have you got to post about? Your vegan tattoos?"

"I certainly could," said The Snowflake. "Some people find them quite interesting."

"Present company excepted," said The Boomer.

Everyone was quiet for a bit, then The Snowflake said, "I'm thinking of having a digital detox. You know, leaving social media, going off-grid and living in the moment."

"Fair enough," said The Baboon, and stole her phone.

# GHOST HUNT

"What do you think happens after we die?" asked The Snowflake.

"A party," said The Boomer.

"That's a very cruel joke," said The Snowflake.

"It wasn't a joke," said The Boomer.

"Let's go on a ghost hunt!" said The Baboon.

The Stuffed Dodo had never been on a ghost hunt, and would have stamped its feet in excitement, had it been able to.

The Boomer told The Baboon, The Snowflake and The Stuffed Dodo to get into his Nissan Micra, and they all drove off to a haunted house.

The journey began normally enough, with a traffic jam on the North Circular Road. But an hour or two later, they were in a deep, dark wood surrounded by howling wolves and banshees. That was Essex for you.

The Baboon wanted to get out and fight the banshees, and The Snowflake had burst into tears. But The Stuffed Dodo was so busy navigating for The Boomer that it didn't have time to notice anything else.

"Are you sure we didn't miss the turning?" The Boomer asked rather crossly.

The Stuffed Dodo wasn't sure at all, but it didn't like being shouted at so it pretended it was. "No, it's definitely this way. Just past the dungeon, the gallows and the plague pit."

"Very well," said The Boomer. "On your head be it."

The Stuffed Dodo didn't like the sound of that. It would have gulped, but it didn't have any spittle. Or a functioning throat.

Before too long, they pulled up outside the haunted house.

It was a crumbling Gothic mansion with grotesque gargoyles leering from the roof.

As they approached the massive oak door, they could hear organ music playing inside. It wasn't a particularly cheerful ditty, thought The Stuffed Dodo. In fact, it was the kind of tune that would go down a storm at a Transylvanian funeral.

The Baboon slammed the knocker up and down repeatedly until a sinister butler opened the door with an ear-splitting CREAK!!! "You rang?"

"Knocked," corrected The Boomer.

"Ah, yes," said the butler. "We were expecting you."

The Stuffed Dodo didn't know why anyone would be expecting them. They hadn't called ahead.

The butler ushered them in to a drawing room. The walls were covered in ancestral portraits of vampires.

"What's the Wi-Fi password?" asked The Snowflake.

"There isn't one," replied the butler.

"Where's the telly?" asked The Baboon.

"You won't be needing that," said the butler, laughing to himself on his way out.

The Baboon, The Boomer, and The Snowflake waited in the gloom while nothing in particular happened.

But for The Stuffed Dodo, it was a completely different matter. Ectoplasmic shapes darted across the room, shouting "BOO!" and "Mwahahaha!". Shimmering skeletons danced in the air – mambos, tangos, cockney knees ups, you name it.

Everything was a bit too lively for The Stuffed Dodo's liking.

Eventually, the butler returned, and switched the lights back on.

"Well, that was dull as ditchwater," said The Boomer.

"Should have gone to the jungle," said The Baboon.

"I've had better nights at the student union," said The Snowflake. Then she noticed that The Stuffed Dodo was looking more frazzled than usual. "What's wrong?"

"I see dead people," said The Stuffed Dodo.

The Snowflake smiled, and said, "Don't worry. It's probably because you're dead too."

The Stuffed Dodo felt its straw shiver.

# WHO'S WHO

"I want to identify as diverse," said The Boomer.

"You can't!" screeched The Snowflake.

"Why not?" asked The Boomer. "I thought anybody could identify as anything."

"Not you! You're ... a privileged, oppressive, straight, white man."

"But am I?" asked The Boomer. "What if I simply decide I'm diverse?"

The Snowflake looked stuck.

The Baboon looked bored.

The Stuffed Dodo felt awkward, so it said, "Why don't we all identify as each other?".

"I would," said The Baboon. "But doesn't it suck to be you?"

"You won't know until you try," said The Stuffed Dodo.

The Boomer turned to The Baboon and said, "Go on, get stuffed!"

The Baboon didn't have much imagination, but decided to give it a go. The Baboon imagined its insides were no longer full of undigested bananas, but elderly straw. It felt itchy and uncomfortable, which put The Baboon in a bad mood. "How do you put up with this all day?"

"I've got used to it," said The Stuffed Dodo. "I got stuffed in 1662, and that was a while ago."

"You're lucky to have lived that long," said The Boomer.

"Yes," said The Stuffed Dodo. "There's a lot to be said for taxidermy."

The Baboon wasn't sure that there was. "Want to identify as me?"

"All right," said The Stuffed Dodo. It scrunched up its eyes and imagined it was swinging through the jungle, hairy arms akimbo.

The sensation of movement was wonderful, and it felt very different to its dreams of flight. Wings took you far higher, but they depended on air currents. With hairy great arms, you were doing all the work yourself, and it felt like you had truly earned your freedom.

"That was fun," said The Stuffed Dodo.

"Eat any good bananas?" asked The Baboon.

"No," said The Stuffed Dodo. "Should I have done?"

"What's the point in being a baboon if you don't eat any bananas?" asked The Baboon in disgusted disbelief.

Things were getting tense, so The Snowflake said, "Okay. Shut up and let me be a boomer for a bit."

She pictured herself overweight, self-satisfied and retired. Her knees hurt, her back ached, and her blood pressure shot up. But her money worries fell away, and so did her principles. Maybe immmigrants really were to blame for everything? Perhaps the unemployed were just a bunch of lazy scroungers? Who knew?

When she snapped back to reality, she felt soiled but much happier. She turned to The Boomer. "Your turn."

"Do I really have to do this?" he asked. "Young people today are the first generation in human history who can report you for bullying whilst stabbing you to death at the same time."

The Snowflake sighed, as The Boomer banged on.

"I suppose I could imagine I was a spoiled, entitled little oik with no life experience and a superior attitude, pedantically correcting other people under the delusion that they can change the world one word at a time." The Boomer paused, then added, "But I can't be arsed."

"Fair enough," said The Stuffed Dodo. "Shall we just identify as ourselves again?"

"Yes," replied the other three.

"Life's much better when you are true to yourself," said The Stuffed Dodo.

"Depends who you are," said The Boomer.

"We're all equal," said The Snowflake.

"I'm not," said The Baboon.

"You're a red-arsed monkey," said The Boomer.

"You're a boring old fart," said The Baboon.

"He is, isn't he?" said The Snowflake.

"He's all right," said The Stuffed Dodo.

"Don't patronise me, you extinct little sod," said The Boomer.

This was a low point in the foursome's friendship, and they almost wondered whether they were suited for each other. But The Stuffed

Dodo had pre-booked them all an away-day by the North Sea, so they all went to the beach and spent an awkward nine hours together.

# THE PUB

The Stuffed Dodo was feeling thoughtful. "You know how we mope about all the time feeling sorry for ourselves, blurting patronising platitudes and quirky nonsense?"

"Yes," said The Snowflake, "I think it's meant to help people escape the miserable reality of their lives and regress to childhood.".

"But what if we didn't?" asked The Stuffed Dodo.

"Good point," said The Boomer. "If people pulled themselves together and got out more, they'd all be much more chipper."

"Mental health is a serious issue," said The Snowflake.

"But isn't that problem?" asked The Boomer. "If people stopped taking themselves so bloody seriously, put an end to their complaining and just got on with stuff, they wouldn't need twee little picture books when they're adults."

"Yes! They could just have a bit of a laugh instead," said the Baboon.

The Snowflake was so irate, she could barely form the words. Her mouth just made soundless shapes for a bit, before the force of her outrage broke through: "People are fragile and toxic attitudes are hurtful. We have to be kinder, and more understanding."

"Boring! Boring! Boring!" said The Baboon.

"Maybe everyone just needs a bit of a laugh," said The Boomer. "Just to take them out of themselves for a bit."

All this had got The Stuffed Dodo thinking. Maybe everyone was a bit stronger than The Snowflake said and you could laugh at them without them falling apart. The Stuffed Dodo decided to put this to the test. "You're a hairy great ape," it told The Baboon. "And you smell."

The Baboon knew all these things were true, but being insulted by a stuffed dodo just made it make lots of "Woo-ah! Ah!" noises and beat up a lamppost.

The Stuffed Dodo was so encouraged, it decided to test out its theory on The Boomer. "You're a silly old fart who bought a house for pence in the nineteen hundreds and retired at fifty. What do you know about anything?"

The Boomer liked being reminded about how cheap his house had been before its value rose to three million. He also loved the fact that he had retired on a massive pension after having a cushy job for life. And it made his face shine gammon-red to know how upset those things made young people feel.

The Stuffed Dodo had rarely seen the Boomer smile. Now, he had – and it was all down to his friendly insult.

The Stuffed Dodo knew that The Sowflake would be a harder undertaking. She was as brittle as an actual snowflake, and always took the wrong end of the proverbial stick. Did The Stuffed Dodo have what it took to make a joke at her expense? It did.

"Your blue hair's not natural, and your pronouns are unpronounceable. Why do you feel entitled to correct other people all the time when your own life is a massive pair of pants?"

The Snowflake's nostrils quivered in outrage, wobbling her nose ring. Did she have a sense of humour? No.

But the Stuffed Dodo didn't care. It decided to boldly go where no one had wanted to go before. "You're hurt all the time. You think the world has got it in for you and needs to be changed. But maybe you just need to cheer up a bit and look outside yourself. That way, there's a small chance someone might like you."

The Snowflake was angrier than she had ever been. She started stomping about, stressing, and wailing. "I've probably got ADHD and I'm possibly on the autism spectrum. I'm neurodiverse too .., and ... and ... lots of things. I need some time on my own."

"Do you really?" said The Boomer. "Why don't we just go down the pub, shoot some pool, and have a laugh?"

The Snowflake was ready to explode in anger. Then she took a deep breath, thought things over for a moment, and said, "You know what, Let's."

THE END

\*\*\*

The world's worst life coach discovers the rules of failure through awkward encounters with eccentric losers. Learn how not to live your life from The Hans Christian Andersen of Incompetence. Get ***How Not To Live Your Life*** by Rich Nash **by clicking here or scanning this QR code:**

# ALSO BY RICH NASH

**H**OW NOT TO LIVE YOUR LIFE by Rich Nash: The world's worst life coach discovers the rules of failure through awkward encounters with eccentric losers. Learn how not to live your life from The Hans Christian Andersen of Incompetence. Get it here:

**COP LIVES PROBABLY MATTER by Rich Nash:** When Cuthbert's jailed for burgling his own home, he takes revenge by penning a wildly insulting crime novel, but the prison's writing tutor just wants him to kill her husband. Get *Cop Lives Probably Matter* by scanning here:

**TRIGGER WARNING by Rich Nash:** After being held hostage in a strip club, Cuthbert discovers that the fate of a disgraced SAS hero lies in his incompetent hands. An edge-of-the-pants thriller where everyone gives a four-figure percentage. Get *Trigger Warning* by scanning here:

**SELF-HINDRANCE by Rich Nash**: Bin the gym, drink your way through "Wet January", re-clutter your home, master a million timewasting tips, and go "From 5k to couch" in this hilarious parody of self-help. Get *Self-Hindrance* by scanning here:

**BLURRED VISIONARY by Rich Nash:** If you're looking for a complete life do-over, a thirty-day loser programme, or a galaxy of dangerously ineffective life hacks, Cuthbert's your man. The entire Legend of Cuthbert Huntsman is available now. Get *Blurred Visionary* and enjoy all three novels in one volume by scanning here:

# ABOUT THE AUTHOR

R ich Nash was senior producer of Warner Bros' and HBO's *Harry Potter Reunion*, which wasn't intentionally funny but was Emmy-nominated, and he was story producer of Netflix's *Stranger Things* feature documentary. His TV shows have featured Meg Ryan, Hugh Grant, Vic Reeves, Jimmy Carr, Joe Wilkinson, Josh Widdicombe, Ross Noble, Sean Lock, Felix Dexter, Katherine Ryan, Bill Bailey, Jonathan Ross, Seann Walsh, David Haye and even John Noakes. He lives in London, read English at King's College, Cambridge, and co-founded the creative AI company Shaggy Dog AI. His TikTok videos as Cuthbert Huntsman, the world's worst life coach, often go viral, with millions of views.

An insensitivity reader was employed to ensure that everything is as triggering as possible. If you are affected by any of the issues raised, there's no helpline - just pull yourself together.

# FREE BOOK

When the world's worst life coach falls out with his AI assistant, it cuts off his oxygen supply, and the race is on to record his final advice for humanity.

Click here to read *Artificial Stupidity – The Dubious Wisdom of Cuthbert Huntsman* for free.

Or scan this:

# FOLLOW CUTHBERT

R ich Nash's alter ego Cuthbert Huntsman is the world's worst life coach and he is on TikTok, YouTube, Twitter/X, Instagram and Facebook.

His website is cuthberthuntsman.com.

Printed in Dunstable, United Kingdom